I Belong to the Buddhist Faith

Katie Dicker and Nisansa De Silva

WAYLAND

First published in 2008 by Wayland

Copyright © Wayland 2008

Wayland
Hachette Children's Books
338 Euston Road
London NW1 3BH

Wayland Australia
Level 17/207 Kent Street
Sydney, NSW 2000

Managing Editor: Rasha Elsaeed

Produced for Wayland by

White-Thomson Publishing Ltd.
210 High Street,
Lewes BN7 2NH

Editor: Katie Dicker
Designer: Clare Nicholas
Editorial consultant: Daniel Owers
Photographer: Chris Fairclough

British Library Cataloguing in Publication Data
Dicker, Katie
  I belong to the Buddhist faith
  1. Buddhism - Juvenile literature
  I. Title II. De Silva, Nisansa
  294.3

ISBN 978 0 7502 5349 9

Printed in China

Wayland is a division of Hachette Children's Books, an Hachette Livre UK company.

Acknowledgements

The author and publisher would like to thank the following people for their help and participation in this book:
The De Silva family, Samantha Palihakkara, Ven. Seelawimala, Richard Jones and all at the London Buddhist Vihara.

The website addresses (URLs) included in this book were valid at the time of going to press. However, because of the nature of the Internet, it is possible that some addresses may have changed, or sites may have changed or closed down since publication. While the author and publisher regret any inconvenience this may cause the readers, no responsibility for any such changes can be accepted by either the author or the publisher.

Disclaimer

The text in this book is based on the experience of one family. While every effort has been made to offer accurate and clearly expressed information, the author and publisher acknowledge that some explanations may not be relevant to those who practise their faith in a different way.

Contents

Going to the vihara

Hi, I'm Nisansa. Today it's Saturday and I've come to the **vihara** with my mum and dad, and my brother, Sachith. We're Buddhists. We've come to give thanks for Lord Buddha's guidance.

We wear white clothes when we visit the vihara as a sign of peace. We've also brought flowers to offer to the Buddha.

The vihara is open every day but we usually go at the weekend. The vihara is the home of some Buddhist monks. It's a place for us to learn more about the Buddha's teachings and to see our Buddhist friends.

The monks wear traditional orange robes and shave their heads like the Buddha did long ago.

Who was the Buddha?

Lord Buddha was a prince called Siddhartha Gautama who lived in India about 2,550 years ago. He had a comfortable life, but he realised sometimes people were unhappy. He wanted to find out how this unhappiness could be avoided.

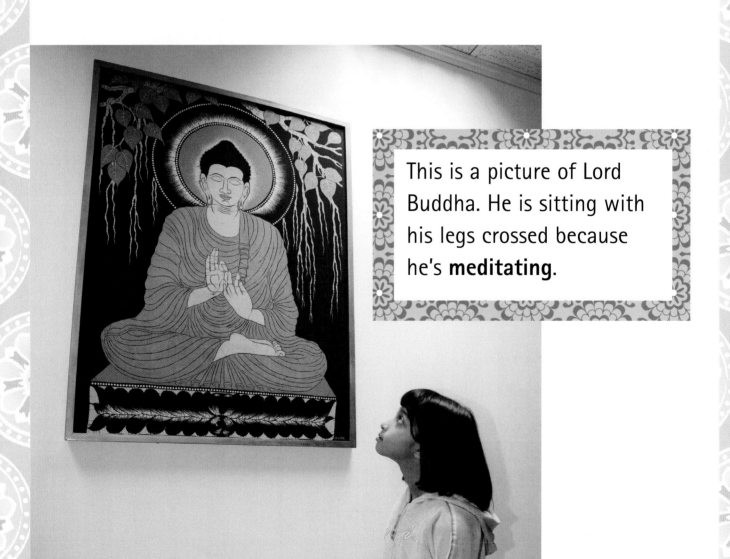

This is a picture of Lord Buddha. He is sitting with his legs crossed because he's **meditating**.

Siddhartha Gautama left his palace and went on a long, difficult journey. One day, while meditating under a bodhi tree, he realised that people can learn to be content with what they have, to avoid feelings of unhappiness. We call this understanding **Enlightenment**.

This bodhi tree at the vihara reminds me of the day Siddhartha Gautama saw the truth and became known as the Buddha – 'the enlightened one'.

The Buddha's teachings

The Buddha started teaching other people new ways of thinking, so they could achieve happiness. His teachings were later written down in an ancient language called Pali. These holy books are known as the **Tripitaka**.

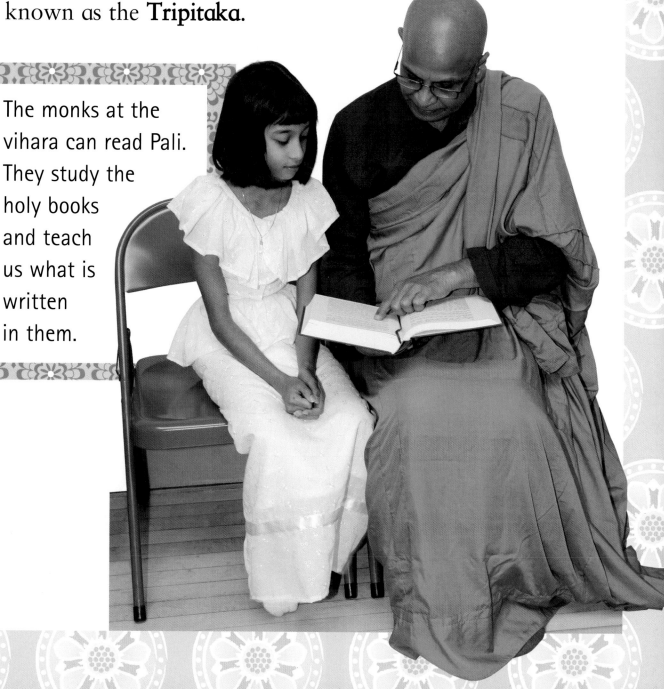

The monks at the vihara can read Pali. They study the holy books and teach us what is written in them.

We all go to the **shrine** room to thank Lord Buddha for his guidance. As Buddhists we think about the **Four Noble Truths**, and how we should behave in our lives to bring happiness to other people, too.

During a **service** at the vihara, the monks **chant** verses from the holy books. We join in with the chanting wishing happiness to everyone.

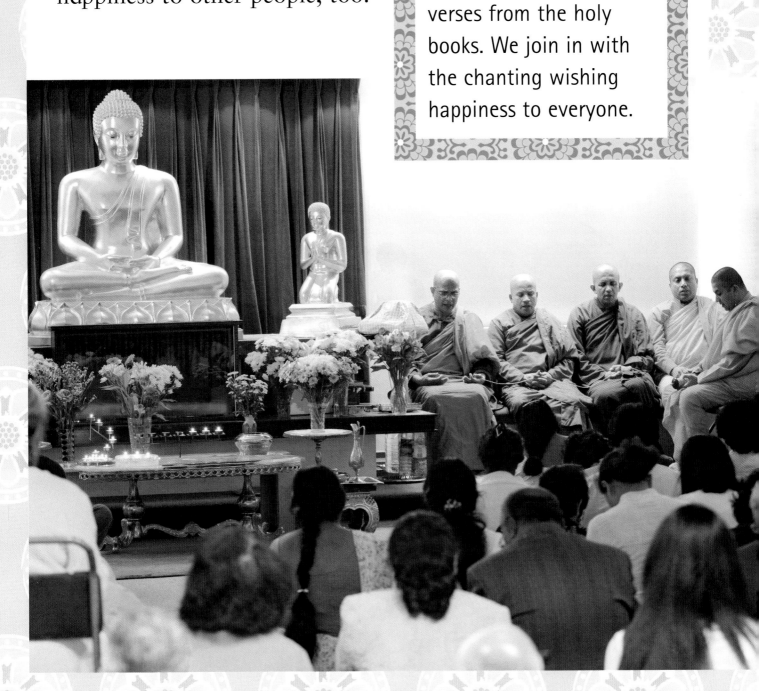

9

Learning about the Buddha

I go to **Dhamma** school at the vihara. We read stories about Lord Buddha and his life. When Siddhartha Gautama left his palace, he lived in the forest before he gained Enlightenment.

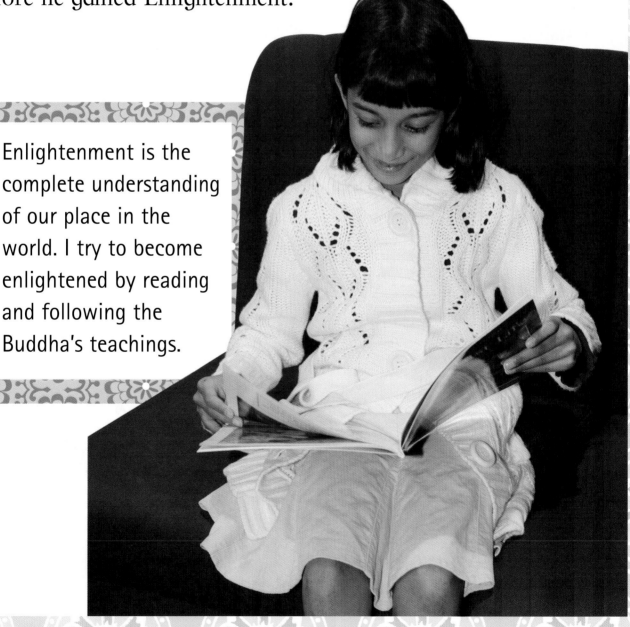

Enlightenment is the complete understanding of our place in the world. I try to become enlightened by reading and following the Buddha's teachings.

The Buddha decided to live as a monk. He did not want to be worshipped as a god. Instead, his teachings are a guide to help people live a better, happier life.

Today, we're learning about how Lord Buddha taught us to be kind and honest and to share things with other people.

Behaving like the Buddha

Buddhists believe that to find happiness we should care for other people. We should also feel comfortable with what we have and who we are. Lord Buddha said that living life in **moderation** would make us happier.

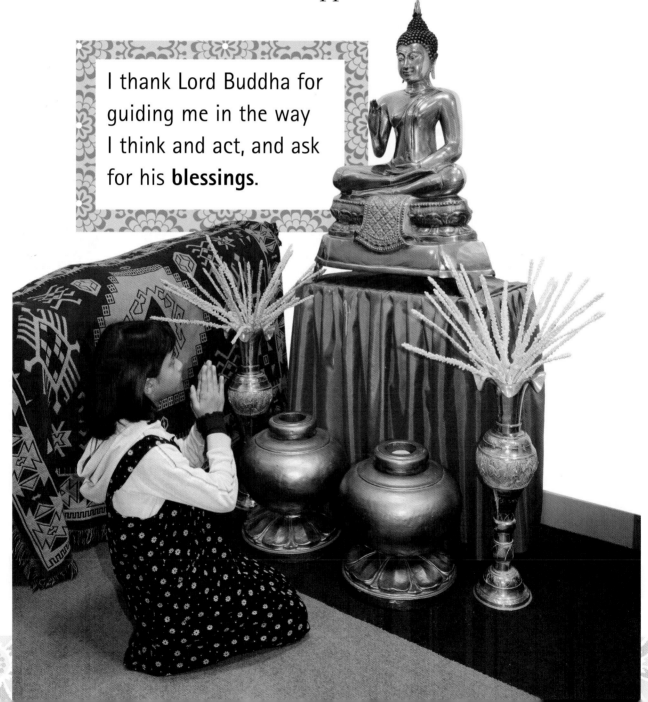

I thank Lord Buddha for guiding me in the way I think and act, and ask for his **blessings**.

We try to meditate like Lord Buddha.
Meditation helps you to become calm and
happy. When we meditate, we train our
minds to concentrate only on good thoughts,
and avoid thinking about bad things.

At home, I practise meditating
with Mum. She teaches
me to be still and
to concentrate
on my breathing.

Living a happy life

I try to follow the Buddha's teachings every day. Sometimes, I feel cross but then I remember bad feelings don't last forever. When I feel happy again, I think how right the Buddha is.

Sachith and I sometimes fall out, but we laugh about it afterwards. We try to bring happiness into the world by not speaking unkindly or harming anyone.

The Buddha showed us how important it is to look after one another. I try to be kind to other people and to show my family, friends and teachers how much I care for them.

I try to help Mum at home. It's good to help other people, so they can have a better day.

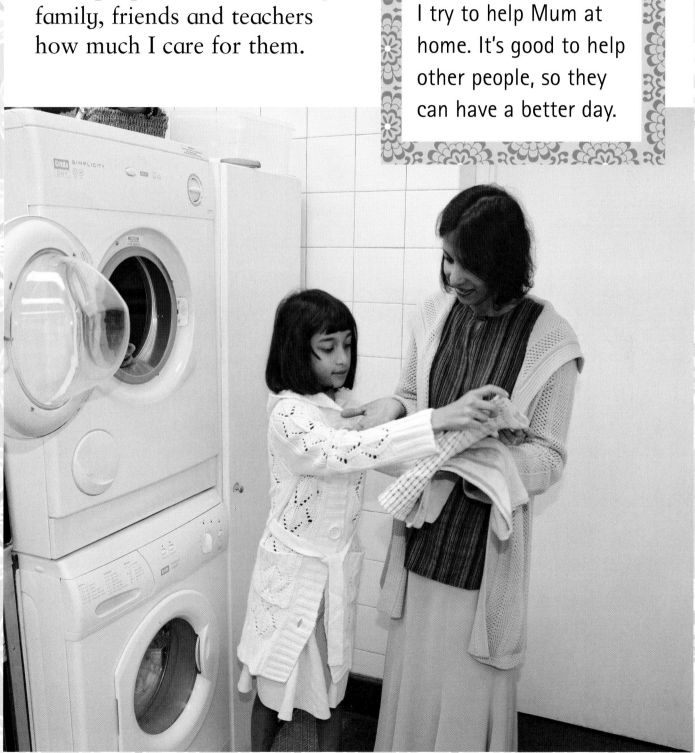

Dana

There's a special service called **Dana** at the vihara every morning. People bring food for the monks. It makes me happy when I give and share what I have with others.

Each Dana ceremony has a different theme. Today, we're giving thanks for what our parents have done for us.

We offer our food to the Buddha first. We also bring flowers, light candles and burn sweet incense. The shrine room is a very peaceful place to show our respect.

Candles remind me that the light of Lord Buddha's teachings will always help me to live a simple, peaceful and happy life.

Food

Lord Buddha taught people to eat in moderation and to be happy with what they receive. For thousands of years, Buddhist monks have followed the Buddha's way of life and only have one or two meals a day.

It's midday and the monks are having their last meal today. They will just drink liquids in the afternoon and evening.

On special days, we have a celebration meal called 'kiribath' that we eat with family and friends. Kiribath is a type of rice cooked in coconut milk – it tastes really good!

These traditional foods are from Sri Lanka where Mum and Dad were born. We often eat kiribath and sweet foods on festival days.

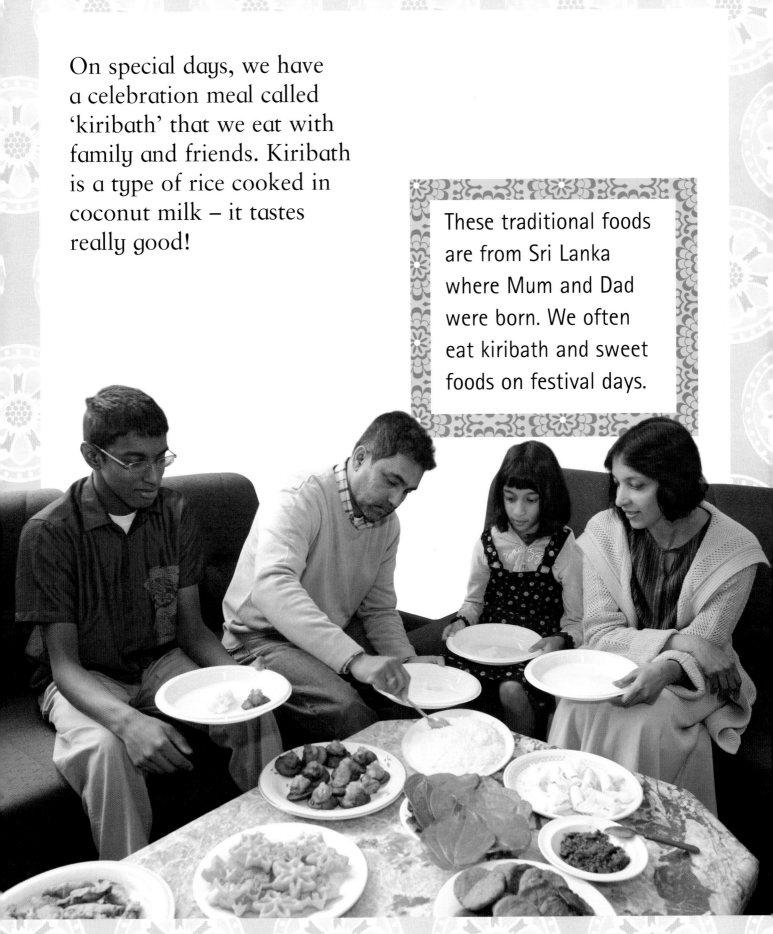

Buddhist festivals

Vesak Day is a celebration that reminds us of Lord Buddha's birth, enlightenment and death. We believe all these important events happened in May, on the day of a full moon.

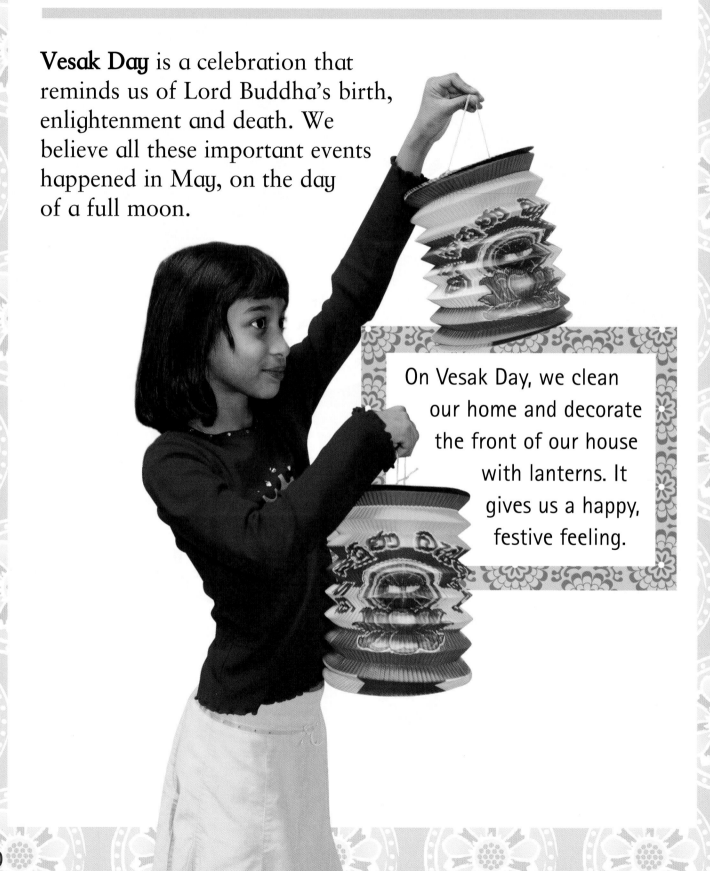

On Vesak Day, we clean our home and decorate the front of our house with lanterns. It gives us a happy, festive feeling.

Days of a full moon are special holy days for us. This is because many important events in **Buddhism** happened on the day of a full moon.

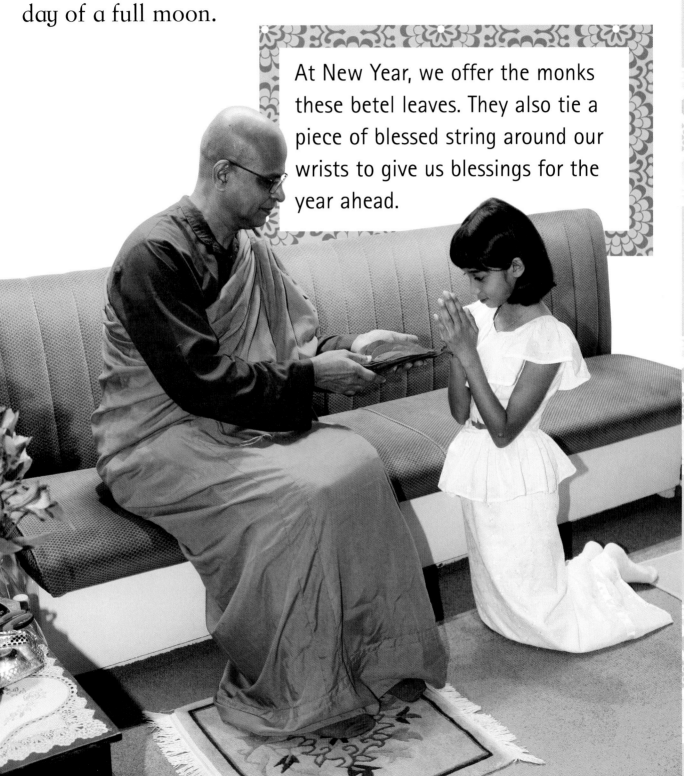

At New Year, we offer the monks these betel leaves. They also tie a piece of blessed string around our wrists to give us blessings for the year ahead.

Glossary and further information

blessing – to look after someone or something.

Buddhism – the Buddhist religion.

chant – to repeat words out loud, often in the same tone.

Dana – the Pali word for giving and generosity.

Dhamma – the Pali word for the Buddha's teachings.

Enlightenment – to see things in their true light, as they really are.

Four Noble Truths – the main teachings of the Buddha about overcoming unhappinness.

meditating – sitting quietly and thinking about something very deeply.

moderation – to avoid having too much or too little of something.

service – a type of ceremony.

shrine – a holy place where people pay their respect, often in front of a statue.

Tripitaka – the holy books full of the Buddha's teachings.

vihara – the home of Buddhist monks.

Did you know?

- Buddhism began in India about 2,550 years ago.
- There are around 350 million Buddhists today, mainly living in Asia.
- There are different types of Buddhists. These include Theravada Buddhists and Mahayana Buddhists.
- Most Buddhist festivals fall on the day of a full moon.

Activities

1. Make your own shrine. Draw a picture of the Buddha and then find some flowers and candles to put around it.
2. Do you know any stories about the Buddha's life? Use books or the internet to find out some of these stories.
3. Write a poem about the Buddhist way of life.

Books to read

- *Buddhist Holy Days* by Brian Knapp, Atlantic Europe Publishing Co Ltd, 2007
- *Buddhist Stories (Storyteller)* by Anita Ganeri, Evans Brothers, 2006

Websites

http://www.buddhanet.net/e-learning/buddhism/storybuddha.htm

This website for primary school children tells the story of the Buddha's life with clear text and illustrations.

http://www.dharmaforkids.com/

A fun introduction to the Buddhist religion for primary school children, featuring stories of the Buddha, Buddhist symbols and online activities.

Organisations

The Buddhist Society
58 Eccleston Square
London
SW1V 1PH

London Buddhist Vihara
Dharmapala Building
The Avenue
Chiswick
London W4 1UD

Buddhist festivals

Buddhist New Year (Jan / Feb / Mar / Apr)
A time to think about how to live a better life. The Buddhist New Year falls in different months in different parts of the world.

Vesak Day (May / June)
A festival to remember the birth, enlightenment and death of the Buddha.

Dhamma Day (July)
A festival to celebrate the Buddha's first teachings.

Sangha Day (November)
A festival to celebrate friendship and to remember Buddhists around the world.

Buddhist symbols

Lotus flower – a reminder of the Buddhist way of life. The Lotus flower grows in the mud at the bottom of a pool, but rises above the surface to become a beautiful flower.

Eight-spoked wheel – the eight spokes are a symbol of the Buddha's teachings, called the Noble Eightfold Path (which forms the fourth Noble Truth). The wheel is a symbol of the cycle of life, death and rebirth.

Index